The Write Way Home

Heather Bennett

BookLeaf Publishing
India | USA | UK

Presentation by *BookLeaf Publishing*

Web: www.bookleafpub.com

E-mail: info@bookleafpub.com

ISBN: 9789360945459

First edition 2024

To Raven: My reason for everything but most importantly my reason for choosing to love myself. You are my greatest gift. I love you to infinity and beyond.

To Ruthie and Louis: For making all of this possible and always loving and supporting me.

To all my relatives and ancestors before me: Watch me break these chains.

ACKNOWLEDGEMENT

There have been many along the way that have supported my work simply by reading my words, my deepest thoughts and fears and have cheered me on with genuine enthusiasm and gratitude.

There have also been those that ignored me all together and have shot down my ideas and taken any chance they could to discourage me from pursuing my dreams.

Thank you all for reminding me who I am doing this for.

PREFACE

The Write Way Home is a compilation of poems I wrote over the past few years while on a cathartic journey home to myself. I had been lost for so long that it felt familiar just blowing in the wind and not really knowing who I was or what I wanted from life. But, I felt this urge in my soul to do something, to be better, to live life in a more meaningful way with intention and gratitude for everything—both the good and well, even the not-so-great. I never really saw myself in the victim mindset but in retrospect, a lot of my behaviors and subconscious beliefs prove it to be so. I was tired of the backstory, beating the drum of not fair and not enoughness and it was time I took my power back. This proved to be a long and weary path. Some days it was all I could do to get out of bed and perform basic household chores and hygiene routines. Writing was sometimes the only way to cure the ruminating thoughts of rejection, abandonment, and failure. Soon I realized those were just that…. thoughts and self-limiting beliefs. I never thought I would be here—writing the preface of my book. But, this is something that I just knew I needed to share.

So please, walk with me as I alchemize anxiety, depression, addiction, judgment, trauma, fear ,and despair into unconditional love, acceptance, compassion, faith, and hope. And stay with me always through the words on these pages and all the love in my heart as I share with you how grace and kindness changed my world.

The Pieces of My Heart

Hundreds of pieces of paper contain my deepest
thoughts
About battles lost and won
And some not even fought
Heartaches, goals, and dreams
Hopes of fixing broken things
Cute li'l notebooks with torn out pages
Filled with poems, musings and some quotes
from sages
Not always a rhyme but in all ways a reason
Some about a lifetime
And some just a season
Some were finished right before the dawn
Some are riveting and some make me yawn
Some are simple and some are complex

Some leave me feeling extremely perplexed
Contemplations of life
what's right and what's wrong
Some make me feel fragile
Some make me feel strong
Scribbled words and scratched out phrases
That one must have been just another one of
those phases
I can't help to think back about what I discarded
The 'not good enough'
The 'done before started'
Addiction and peril … and the ADHD
Always in AWE of the way that God created me.
Some filled with sadness
Some filled with rage
But still so much love in every ME filled page
Bar napkins, envelopes, and a piece of cardboard
box
Some of them are epic and some of them are
flops
Not all of them make sense
Nothing really does.
Some have deep meaning
Some are just because
Hundreds of pieces of paper in cute li'l books
Shoved in boxes, in closets, in corners and in
nooks.

It's Okay

It's ok so much time has passed.
That you promised me forever but gave a love
that didn't last.
It's ok to feel hurt, pain, sorrow, and grief,
Guilt, shame, hatred, jealousy, and deceit …
It's ok you feel anxious, empty, and blue this is
the exact same way I felt about you.
I took all of that and stayed way too long
Transformed it into something
That I thought was love
Convinced myself it was right
when everything was wrong.
A love you didn't reciprocate
A song you'd never sing
A love that I gave to myself
That only your absence could bring
It's ok you can't find words to say
how you truly feel.
No need to wonder now if this was ever really
real

You could have asked that I be patient
or said you needed time
Instead you shut down and ignored me
pretending everything was fine.
You could have told me that you were confused
instead of keeping me
Guessing, feeling broken and used
Instead you sat and watched me pouring from
my empty cup
Too tired to keep trying
Too stubborn to give up
There was a time you said you wanted to see me
thrive
but instead you created a world in which I could
barely survive.
This can't be the kind of thing that you call love
as within, so without
As below, so above
I clawed my way out of hell many times before
but that pales in comparison to walking out your
door.
I need no excuses, reasons, or apologies
No validation will fix all the things you did to
me.
I held space in my heart and trusted you for
years
But now your last words just ring in my ears…
I am done with you.
Over it.

Finished.
Done.
I thought you hung the moon but you blinded
like the sun.
But now you see I am finally over it too.
And I hope you fall in love with someone just
like you.

No Words

Let words become meaningless
No need to make a fuss
The this and that
and tit for tat
If and when
and there and then
The who, what, why?
Should we laugh or do we cry?
When words don't matter
And there's no mindless chatter
No labels or names
No more silly games
When the letters don't even make sense on their
own
What becomes of the place that you once called
home?
Will it make us stronger or make us weak?

You see no need for tongue in cheek
And nothing you say but all that you do
Not words but deeds are what define you
So then just imagine what we could become
When we finally realize that we are all one
When our only language comes from the heart
And not a single word can tear us apart
Instead one that unites within and above
Not a word or a feeling
It is just simply love.

Choose Love

Choosing not to love because you've been hurt
is like being so hungry that you can't eat.
Like trying to run without having two feet
When winded, do we not stop and gasp for air?
Remember in love and war, nothing is fair
When dehydrated sometimes, we can only take
sips
suck on ice chips
Or get an IV stick
And though the perils of heartbreak sometimes
play on repeat
like a B side record that won't stop the beat
I often wonder what kind of person I would be
If I stopped living my life
my way
Just for me
I survived many a days with a broken heart
If I ever stopped loving I remembered to restart
Picking up pieces with a dustpan and mop
Some pieces cut deep but the bleeding would
stop
And sometimes a stitch was needed to mend
But the real healing I know always came from
within
So when the nights seem too lonely

What will you do?
Don't poison yourself with pills or with brew
Remind yourself that you are a gem
More precious than diamonds
And much rarer than them
Don't choose to be angry bitter or cold
Fall in love with you
C'est la vie to the old
Love and fear cannot coexist
So, please choose love
On this I insist
Love all those pieces right back into place
With compassion and kindness
Then comes Grace.

More Choices

Earth can be a prison or it can be a school.
You can be the teacher or you can be the fool.
Either way, you get to choose.
Be the artist or be the muse.
When you open your eyes you begin to realize
that all along you had the tools.

You can create worlds or you can watch them
crumble.
Sink or swim. Shout or mumble.
Firm grip or clumsy fumble.
A quiet hum. A roaring rumble.

Thoughts, beliefs, and perspective.
What you emit will be reflected.
So send out all the love you can.

Be grateful for everything you have. Even the
conflict—because it won't last.
Be mindful. Be grateful. Be loyal and faithful.
But fill your cup first. There's infinite
knowledge to quench your thirst.
Then pour for others from the center of your
heart.
After every ending there's always a new start.

The Path Less Taken

I went from shimmy shimmy cocoa puff
To puff puff pass
From God, I hope they like me
To they can all kiss my ass
Optimistically thinking the glass is half full
To vodka in my water bottle
A tasty beverage before school
Went from anything broken I was sure that I
could fix
To selling my soul just to get my next
Straight laced
Straight A's
To just straight blitzed
Blacked out out back
To screaming, shouting, throwing fits

When did I stop dreaming and believing in the
good
And start acting like a badass
Wishing a mother fucker would
It's not like my parents gave up in the midst of
peril
They never fathomed rearing a child so
unabashedly feral
Homecoming queen to methamphetamine
Hallucinogenics felt like home to me
From baby doll dresses and bobby socks
To orange jumpsuits and county cell blocks
Southern Baptist to agnostic
Damn I think your girl might've lost it
Stargazer
dopamine craver
Poppin pills
Please God save her
Some say I never amounted to much
I say they were too scared to fuck up
Too scared to fail and even more scared to
succeed
If you ask me I'll tell you I have everything I
need
Sure I took the road less traveled
Kicked up some dust spun up some gravel
Stayed too long and tried too hard
Not very often I'd let down my guard
At the end of the day it wasn't a waste

Hard lessons were learned in feverish haste
Desperately grasping as the mask began to slip
To zero fucks given
I ain't hidin' shit.

Be Still and Know

I want to paint.
I want to scream.
I'm wide awake but it feels like a dream.
I want to laugh. I want to cry.
I can't explain. Please don't ask why.
I want to dance. I want to write.
Here to heal: Born to fight.
I want to travel. I want to draw.
I want to be able to let go of it all.
I want to speak and my words be heard.
Authentically weird, it's all so absurd.
It's hard to articulate all that I know.
Just take a peek now through the windows of my
soul.
Strange or familiar??
You want to go home??

Don't worry darling, you aren't alone.
Talk if you want or don't make a sound.
Soon you will see that we share common
ground.
We aren't so different—you and me.
When was the last time you truly felt free?
When was the last time that you really felt
connected?
Not alone in a crowd.
Not lost. Not rejected...
Your soul can't be nourished if you don't open
up.
Remember: you cannot pour from an empty cup.
What do you see from your point of view?
Do you see me? Do you see you?
Something you admire or something that
offends?
Do things ever look the same
from the outside peering in?
I know it all seems a bit too bizarre... you wake
up one day and wonder who you are.
How did you get here and where did you go?
Who noticed the difference?
Who's resisting the flow?
Indeed there's a lesson behind every event; the
hardest part is not knowing what any of it meant.
Or why it had to happen …
When does the pain subside?

If the road is less traveled then why's it such a
bumpy ride?
Focus on the future—nothing less than what's
sublime.
Trust all answers come to you in
perfect divine time.
Til then get lost in some adventures. Have fun
and follow joy.
You've proven time and time again that you
refuse to be destroyed.
Sick for home and battle weary
You don't know what's not yours to carry
Regardless of this you won't be fazed
Bruised, not broken, somehow minimally
unscathed.
I always say a li'l prayer for you
I always knew you'd find your way.
So, given the opportunity this is what I have to
say
I see you out there trying
even on your darkest day,
People all around you but you know you're on
your own
But, even on those lonely nights
darling you never were alone.
And still, you believe in the good of mankind.
It's ok to feel like you've lost your damn mind.
Sometimes we feel stuck like everything is
screwed

But, when choices are slim, always choose
gratitude.
Choose love.
Be patient
and always trust the process.
Don't focus on what's left to do
Just focus on the progress.
Look in the windows again and you'll see;
I am you and you are me.
Keep your head held high
You shine bright like the sun
Remember me friend
For we are one.

Just Another Day

As another day slowly creeps towards its end
I'm so far from where I started
I'm not sure where I began
I've been running around in circles
Like a stray dog chasing its tail
And I don't give myself enough credit
For all the times I didn't fail.
Nothing new. No other way.
Nothing special… just another day.
Then all of life's little worries and trivialities
Seemed to disappear like the setting sun
And made it easier to believe
That good people still really do exist
The bad times never stay
Silently I make a wish
For just another day

A shooting star that fell too soon
Lights up the sky with help from the moon
And millions of stars I see with my eyes
It's the brightest one
Nothing comparable in size
That lonely star that shined so bright
Twinkled back
alone in the night
My mind goes blank
As I fall to my knees
"Thank you, God."
I have everything I need
To create, to dream, to laugh, to play
I am grateful God for just another day.
So friends please, let me tell you this
If you got a shit-show
And you ordered bliss
if your today wasn't all that great
A crick in your neck
or you woke up too late
If you didn't sleep
not a single wink
If your mind is racing
and you can't even think
If peace of mind was fleeting and dreadful
thoughts consumed your head
If you forgot why you walked in that room
Or even what the hell you just said
Take a moment

Stop and breathe
No worries here
Just allow …
And receive
Eventually I think you'll find
A calm within
A quiet mind
Inhale
Exhale
And slowly say
Thank you, God
For just another day.

These Keys

Far be it from me to set you free
These keys are not mine to hold
The cage you are in
doesn't seem to condemn
For it's lined with silver and gold
And the clothes that you wear
Not a tatter or tear
So what is the fuss all about?
Your belly is full
And your bed comfortable
Still you whine complain and pout
You wither and writhe
From the pain deep inside
Too hard to face it
Too easy to hide
Thoughts and memories
You can't seem to shake
No elixir or pill
Will ease your heart's ache
Don't let the emptiness drive you insane
And leave you alone
Guilt ridden with shame
Ruffle those feathers and let out your call
Are you afraid you will soar or afraid you will
fall?

Close your eyes and quiet your mind
Be grateful for living and soon you will find
This prison, this cage, this place you call home
Is locked with limitations and fear of unknown
Break free from your mind and
Get out of your head
Use those feathers for flying
And not for your bed
I can't tell you much more
But I can promise you this
On the other side of fear
Is a lifetime of bliss.

The Silence In Between

The song doesn't make you sad anymore just
because you stopped listening to it.
The lyrics are still the same
And the feelings never really went away
So, when you're ready turn it on again
And play it on repeat
Until the truth is just nothing but words
That still knock you off your feet
And while you're down there sit awhile
Cry or scream or simply be
Until the past becomes a familiar tune
And the melody and harmony softly fill the
room
When you come back home to your own being
And your soul feels light enough to fly and sing
Remember the words and the verses yet heard
Your soul knows this song by heart
So, should you stumble upon the words
Or you can't tell the end from the start
When the pain starts to leave
And you can finally breathe

Its ok to let it all out or
Even sing a bit off key
For nothing sounds quite as sweet
As a being that knows their truth
And remembers the silence in between
That unites us with what was our youth.

The One That Got Me Stirring

He watched
As she stared down into her coffee cup stirring
as if she was trying to tunnel through to the
other side of the world …
"Hey."
She didn't even blink.
"Heeeyy. Look at me. Up here …" he said. He
slowly reached over and gently lifted up her chin
so her eyes would meet his.
Such sweet, kind eyes … They thought about
one another.
She glanced at him as tears filled hers.
He winced.
And for a brief moment sadness met sadness.
"Tell me," he said.
"Please."
She inhaled sharply.
He whispered: "How can someone who's known
so much pain continue to love so much?"
"Because," she said,
"That's all I've ever known. Love and pain. Pain
and love."
He didn't seem surprised but maybe a bit …
impressed almost.

"What about fear?" He asked quietly in a rather boyish tone.

She looked up at him. Everything stopped. Everything was still. And for a brief second he could swear he saw a fire ignite in her eyes…. There was this … shift

Like an invisible force pulled her shoulders back and then she sat up straight. And still she stirred but oh so slowly now …. "You know…" she stirred …

she inhaled deeply,

held her breath for a few seconds

and as she exhaled her stirring halted.

She gently placed her spoon down, folded her hands into a praying position in front of her and locked eyes with him once again.

The air between them reminded him of the vapor coming off a hot asphalt road in the middle of August … she leaned in. Just enough.

Fear is kindling. She said. Her voice cracked a bit at first. Ahem (she cleared her throat and sat up further making sure her words were clear) Fear is the catalyst that ignites anything beautiful … anything detrimental… anything that proves you have a soul. There will always be contrast in everything. Always. That's the beauty of it. You have to be bigger than fear. See, if you don't learn how to dance in the flames you'll end up getting burned every time."

"Wow," he said, "That's powerful."
She grinned a half grin and gently sat her spoon
down on her saucer. She relaxed a little and with
a kind smile, she asked, "What about you? What
are you afraid of?"
He replied, "You know I spent half of my life
trying to convince myself I wasn't scared of shit
and if you had asked me that even a couple of
months ago I would have said exactly that."
"And what about now?" she asked.
He shrugged a big shrug and playfully asked,
"Care to dance?"

Cuppa Joe

Sun streams in across my face
As I pull the curtain to light up this place
The dust is back and the floors need swept
10-step coffee day … I just sat and wept
Then I pulled myself together again as the coffee
began to brew
I pour a cup and take a sip and for a moment feel
brand new.
The things I choose to worry about seem a bit
cliche
First world problems suffocate and still I
wait for a new day
A day where everything starts to make sense
A day when there's no reason to take offense
A day where we all look at one another
And finally realize that we are sisters
We are brothers
We are fathers and we're mothers
No relation to each other
Except that we are not divided
Share a smile, a hug, and our pain is subsided
All we want is to be loved and accepted
In a world that hates and leaves us feeling
rejected

So when you take some time to sit and think
whether it's wine or just a cuppa joe you drink
When you can see the hurting human in others
and not label them friend or foe.
When life hands you lemons make lemonade
And share with another soul
It may seem simple and a little mundane
But maybe for someone else
This might just be that brand new day.

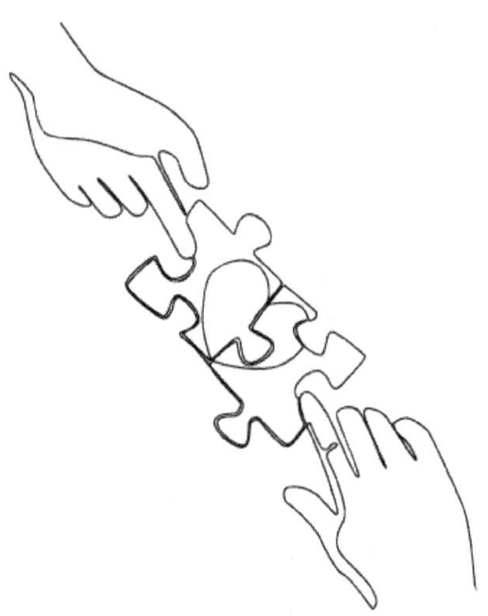

Eyes Wide Shut

In this backwards society
All of us seem to be
Tormented emotionally
blindfolded, following
ever so faithfully
We must learn to question
every damn thing
Voting for crooks without reading the books
Choices are based on empty promises and looks
Left wing, right wing, it's the same damn bird
Once they've taken their seats they don't hear a
word
Elected officials don't care
About you and me
Still we sit by hoping things turn out so
differently
Silently watching history repeat

while hard working citizens continue to get beat
In order for any of us to truly be free
We have to take back our power eventually
False prophets merely profiting
We fill their wallets abundantly
The stench of their lies just wafting so pungently
It spews from their mouth like a ravenous puss
As they snub their noses
They look down on all of us
Does the scent of fear
mean that the end is really near?
Some of you still care about affiliation
When their entire agenda is world domination
Distracted by media and the kind of watch that
adorns their wrist
Time is just a concept
Are you getting the gist?
When protecting and serving is done so in vain
And conspiracy theorists start to sound sane
When the truth seems impossible to actually
discern
I implore you all to please wake up and learn
This world is tainted by all of our 'isms
Their covert ways of creating a schism
Em Ploy simply means to cause deceit
But it's too late to learn this when we are under
6 feet
I want to shout
I want to roar

I want to kick their venomous asses right out the
door
United we stand, divided we fall
All for one and one for all
In God we trust—but we need to do more
What the hell are we fighting each other for??
We need to KNOW and not just believe
Because there's a LIE smack dab in the midst of
belief
The things that you do and places you go
The morals you stand for
The the love that you show
Open your eyes
Take a look deep inside
Someday soon I hope that we all realize
All that we plant is all that we sow
You must tend to the soil for your garden to
grow
If what comes around goes around
Then what will you get?
Even flowers bloom brighter when the soil's
mixed with shit
May the words by mouth and thoughts of mind
bring inspired action
and all three align
Freedom to choose
free to decide
I wish you the courage
to not run and not hide.

Love thy neighbor as you love yourself
sometimes it's good to put your pride on the
shelf
Much better than laying your life on the line,
monsters in suits don't care what's yours and
what's mine
The poor get poorer and the sick never heal
We've got to wake up and see what is right and
what's real.
We are the creators of our own destiny
Don't ever let them tell you who and what you
should be.
Nothing inside is as bad as external
We are infinite beings
Our soul is eternal
You have the courage and now is the time
You must face your darkness
In order to shine.

FEAR: Forget Everything And Rise

My life as an epic poem
Full of comedies and
Tragedies
Lost at sea
What about me
I cry when I'm happy
laugh when I'm afraid
Occasional stories of the dragons I've slayed
The skeletons in my closet
The monster under my bed
All just a mirror of the nightmares replaying in
my head
Running from my shadow with a monkey on my
back
Hanging by a thread but could use a li'l slack
But at the end of the day

Like all of them before
Truth remains
Fear subsides
And I'm not running anymore.

My Girl

There once was a beautiful girl
Who believed in the good of the world.
She didn't care about diamonds or gold
She only wanted someone to love and to hold.
She gave and she poured from her own empty
cup
She never once questioned
And she never gave up.
She never once sat and thought "poor pitiful me"
She had faith and trust in what's meant to be.
She never once let life make her bitter
She loved fearlessly and vowed to never be a
quitter.
Oh she would quit things not good for her soul
But if the world tried to bury her she'd just
climb right out that hole.
A woman like this is so hard to find.
Authentic, courageous, and one of a kind.

And no matter how far away and no matter the
time
I will always be grateful for a love this sublime.

Leave Me Gently

"Leave me gently," she cried.
Let's revel in the
DELICIOUSNESS
of it all
We took a leap of faith
Let us not despise the fall
Let's be grateful for the
Opportunity to share such a
BEAUTIFUL LOVE
Wild, adventurous and free
As fleeting as it was
Leave me knowing we will find our way
back to us again
One small prayer—our parting gift
Dear God
Please
Amen

Leave me kindly, she begged
Help me sweep up the pieces of our shattered
dreams
And put them in a box with a bow
Up high on a shelf—the darkest corners of my
mind where most are afraid to go
And in another hundred years

Or maybe in the blink of an eye
We'll take them down and dust them off
Make art. And laugh. And cry.
Let's spread all those tiny pieces
Across the horizon in the sky
Like a million eternal moonlit nights
Where planets and stars stay aligned.

The Long Hard Look

One day I woke up
I woke up one day and realized the life I was
living was a lie.
One day I woke up and chose myself.
I woke up one day and decided, from the depths
of my soul, I would not settle for anything less
than authentic.
And "authenticity" oh that seemed so vague and
terribly casual and honestly even a bit blasé.
But this is the word that stuck out in my mind.
This was the word that synchronistically started
popping up everywhere.
This was the word that made it through the mud
and the muck of the self-inflicted tortured mind.

Authenticity broke free from the mire and began to bloom despite it all.

Authenticity was the lotus flower fertilized with sheer will and determination to live a life worth waking up to everyday—to experience love and emit kindness—and to want more of it over and over again.

To drink up every last delicious drop and want more and more and more as if gluttony was never a sin.

It was the broken record that played on repeat. That catchy tune that gets stuck in your head but you only know the Melody and can't quite grasp the next verse.

What does it mean to be AUTHENTIC?

Put simply, authenticity means you're true to your own personality, values, and spirit, regardless of the pressure that you're under to act otherwise. You're honest with yourself and with others, and you take responsibility for your mistakes.

Well sh!t … this may take a little more sorting out than we planned for.

You see, I realized that I'd been living life inauthentically when I did not speak up for myself or others because I did not want to rock the boat or stir the pot.

I was not being authentic when people tried to form me into something that would only be good for their agenda—not allowing me room to grow into what I was meant to become on my own terms but I stayed too long and tried too hard anyway and that was inauthentic.
I was not being authentic when I said I was fine and I clearly wasn't.
I was being inauthentic when I allowed myself to be treated as a handmaid when what I really needed was a hand that made things easier and better together with someone who cared ABOUT me not about what I could do for them.
There were so many ways I was not authentic—to those I cared about and most importantly to myself.
And on that day I woke up and discovered this inauthentic shell of the person I thought I was standing in there in my shoes and my clothes.
My reflection was so unfamiliar.
Eyes wide shut and oblivious to the blatant deceit that had become my entire existence.
So, I stared blankly into the mirror and it was like peeking into oblivion until finally I opened my eyes to the truth
I looked deep into my soul for the first time in a long time and asked myself
Who am I?
Who have I become?

Who was I to begin with?
What is the point of any of this?
Why am I here?
What is my purpose?
What do I want from any of it and why do I
want it?
How can I become the best version of me and
live my life on purpose?
And I heard a quiet whisper:
Be still. Be still and know that I am God. And
the kingdom of heaven is within you.
Open your heart and believe. Believe in yourself
for I am within you. I will never deny you. And I
will never leave you alone.
And as I stood before myself I realized I also
stood before God and I began to cry tears of
quicksilver that seemed to wash away all the
remnants of who I ever thought I was. I stood
there shrouded in grace and compassion
knowing I am not alone. I never have been. I am
the breaker of chains and the voice of the
voiceless. I will not waste my time roaring but
my words will forever echo. And I knew I was
looking at myself through the wrong lenses all
this time simply because I always wanted to see
myself through other people's eyes.

The Reasoning

I've always been one of those "EVERYTHING for a REASON" types of people. But, sometimes life just shakes you up and throws you down and cracks you open one too many times. And, it's in this broken state of irreparable existence when rock bottom becomes your all too familiar modern day Hotel California that you have to find YOUR reason in the HAPPENING. That tough shell of protection you created just crumbles away revealing the lost terrified child chasing tarnished silver linings, barefoot, down some ole dirt road in Oklahoma on a hot summer afternoon. They've run so far for so long they found respite exploring the caves from the darkest corners of your mind to deep down in the pit of your gut. Crawling on hands and knees careful as to not leave traces of prints. Quietly wincing from every move wanting to quit but not willing to stop. Finally collapsing they Nestle deep within using the last piece of your soul as a security blanket. The darkness envelopes them and the memories of loss and betrayal feels like porcelain against hot skin. All the pain within and without sings them to sleep like some somber lullaby. Are they lost or are they hiding? Alone in the darkness can be a scary place. But, for some it becomes a sort of safe haven where no one can see their red puffy tear-filled eyes. A place where no one will look and no one can take the last bit of your soul that you aren't willing to let go of. A place where the voices, now comforting, make much more sense and the cold feels welcoming against a sweat-soaked shirt. The nightmare of reality is still but a dream you can't fully emerge from. And as you move amidst the drudgery of day to day life you wrestle with matters of the head and the heart so robotically you're distracted from feeling and thinking and doing things that you don't even notice until autopilot malfunctions. Your fuel—depleted. You can't get into gear and not even roadside services can reach you. How did you get here? What will you do? Lost and alone in the middle of nowhere and no one can hear your screams. You close your eyes, breathe deep and release. And then, from the darkest corner of your mind you hear a whimper. A weak, defeated voice within that's called out for help for so long their breath is shallow and their voice is meek. You immediately follow the cries with your heart. A long winding road where all light fades away. The passage narrows and the moon hides behind the clouds. With every twist and every turn you begin to wonder if you'll find your way back out of this. The path disappeared long ago; replaced by a great stone wall covered in thorns and needles and razor wire. You can't tell where Hell ends and Heaven begins if there really even is such a place. But you use it to guide you deeper within and and like the witch and the wardrobe you find a portal to break through. This journey feels like a lifetime but you can't quit now. You're closer than ever now. Your breath is the only thing you can see. But you feel a warm presence there in the nothingness so you call out but there is no answer. Is this real or just a dream? Exhausted you collapse and slide down the wall. A small hand reaches out—be careful, don't fall. A shaky voice whispers, "are you looking for this?" And hands you the tattered blanket held together by just a stitch. This poor lost soul is

your shadow. A once sweet and innocent child
so lost and neglected they buried themselves in
the coldest darkest corner of your being. You
have to find them! You have to reach them.
Uncover them. Wrap them in your love and just
sit with them. They are you and you are them.
Do you love you enough to trust you? Can you
learn to love yourself, not in spite of yourself,
but FOR YOURSELF. Can you become your
own beacon of light in the darkness? You have
to save yourself. Over and over and over again.
You have to allow yourself to find yourself and
save yourself. You have to roll up your sleeves
and crawl down in it in order to … live, to
breathe, to BE. THIS is your survival mode.
This is your calling, your purpose, your reason.
Once you help yourself clean up the wreckage of
a life you built caused by loving and trusting and
hoping and faith … once you pick yourself up,
dust yourself off, and climb your way back out
of the trenches for the (God only knows)
umpteenth time… You LEARN. Yes, you learn.
Your karma becomes your dharma—it's all just a
lesson that turns into a blessing. Pay attention
closely because now the real work begins. For,
none of this really matters at all if you don't use
this newfound magical light to shine upon others
long enough to show them that they too can be
their own heroes. But Darling first you must do

this for you. You will learn that each and every
person, place, and thing in this life brings with
it a chance for you to practice patience, love, and
kindness … and, most importantly, a reason to
practice gratitude. Live a life that warms hearts
and brings smiles not only for others but for
YOU, your shadow, for that innocent little inner
child. Be the person you always needed when no
one else showed up. Give yourself the love you
give away. Hold that frightened child inside and
let them know they are safe, they are loved, and
they are protected. BE someone they would be
proud of. Gather the fragments of your soul you
find along the way and stitch them back together
with the threads of good intentions that turned
into disappointment and heartbreak. The latter
does not matter anymore. The good intentions
still remain. Cover yourself up for now you are
whole again and now the healing can begin. You
are not alone. You never have been. You are one
in the oneness of everything there ever was and
will be. Diamonds were once lumps of coal
placed under immense amounts of pressure …
Now, see how rare and precious they are? See,
how bright they shine? Don't let life make you
bitter, cold, and cruel. Go within and you'll
never go without. Everything may not happen
for a reason but finding your reason is
everything.

Good Grief

Grief is like gum stuck to the bottom of your only pair of shoes. But there is no way to scrape it off or wipe it away. No matter how hard you try there's always a bit of sticky residue that when you least expect it reminds you that something somewhere changed the way you walk.

I have lost too many people to addiction. Some say it's a choice. Some say it's selfish. Some say it's a disease. Some say it's incurable. And I'm here to tell you that it's all of these until it's not.

See, I have found (for me) that addiction was a way to mask or keep from dealing with painful things that I hated myself for. Something to make me feel or make me not feel. Numbness hurts more than any pain I have ever experienced.

The crazy thing is that addiction doesn't care how much money you have in your bank account or even if you have a bank account. Addiction doesn't do a credit check and it doesn't make you take a personality test or an IQ test. It doesn't care what your profession is, how many sq ft your house is, whether you rent or own or call the streets your "home." It doesn't care what kind of car you drive … four wheels, two wheels, or heel toe express matters not to addiction. It will always be there for you. Waiting …. watching … stalking.

The cure only works one day at a time.

So, if you or someone you love is "battling" addiction and it seems to be winning … surrender. Everyday. Surrender. Love yourself and/or them a little bit extra. Don't enable. Don't abandon. Just slow down and know with enough love you will prevail. It takes a village. It really does. And, if you aren't part of the solution you are part of the problem. You cannot keep doing the same thing and expect a different outcome without calling it insanity. Don't wait to live your life. Don't wait to forgive yourself and love yourself.

The same God who created the universe thought the Earth wouldn't be complete without every single soul He placed on it. And He created each one of us in His image … maybe we can all find a little more grace and compassion and kindness. Like Him.

Do Overs

When you need someone to talk to
But you don't know what to say
And it doesn't seem quite fair
To share with others your bad day
When you want to kick and scream and shout
Or take a scalding hot shower
and cry it all out
When there's no more tears
And the rivers run dry
When you hurt so much you just want to die
When you hold so tight that you lose your grip
Or walk too carefully… it's then that you slip
When you can't make sense of what's up or
down
When you fake a smile while your heart wears a
frown
When you'd give anything to just restart this day
In hopes you'll eventually get out of your own
way
Do something different have a little fun
Dance in the kitchen
Sit in the sun
An attitude of gratitude is all that it takes
To find self love, compassion, and grace
Forgive yourself for being unkind

For using harsh words
And not letting you unwind
Just breathe, darling, breathe
Let yourself feel alive
Don't try so hard and stop trying to hide
Take a walk and let go
With every step every stride
What you are seeking can be found within
There is no finish line
You can always start again.

The Edge

I screamed your name into the ocean last night
Wishing that would somehow bring you back to
me again
Instead the waves just roared and crashed
Scattering shreds of faded memories like
confetti in the sand quickly washed away by
glimmers of contented despair

I stood at the edge of the ocean and screamed
your name
A lowly guttural primordial growl that seemed
to start in my toes
And felt as if it would rip my intestines out as it
made its way out of my mouth

The waves just enveloped it all and took it back
out to sea
And I'm just standing here frozen
Hoping somehow you'll find your way back to
me.

Never Again

I see pain in the eyes of another
Is it just a mere reflection of mine
How can they look and not see
how fallen apart I really must be
Trying to hold it all in in one place
while invisible tears fall down my face
they never know because they leave no trace
My silent cries
my soul survives
one more day
of dying inside
It hurts so bad
that I can't just be sad
the smiles and jokes
and laughter just chokes
As I writhe in silence
from emotional violence and self deprivation
I seek isolation
all the while wanting
to be a part of it all
To help soften their fall and soothe their soul
to Hold their hand
as we take a stroll
Because I want them to know
that I've been there before

and being alone
is like casting a stone
and sinking beneath the oceans waves
when everyone stares but nobody saves
I'll dive down to the bottom for them
because I don't want anyone to feel alone like
that
never again.

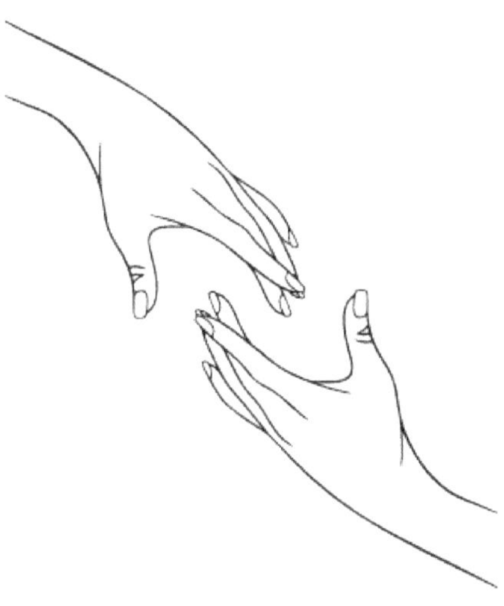

No Place Like Home

She was homesick for a place she wasn't sure
existed
She doesn't even remember how it felt to be
alive in that space
But more than anything else her soul craved it
The walls adorned in tones of comfort and
inspiration
Perfectly curated art that spoke a language only
she could understand
Curtains of lace hung from windows reminders
of the veil between two worlds
A garden where she planted seeds of hope and
Gently pulled the weeds of broken dreams from
fertile soil

To sit in the sun again in that place
Or maybe for the first time
The cool breeze gently caressing her sun kissed
face
Worry, grief, anxiety, and fear
All just words on a tear stained page of
yesterday's book.

The Last Goodbye

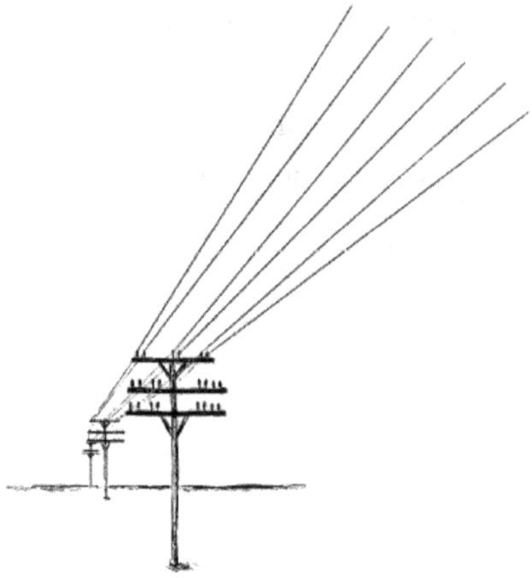

How many times can I pace this floor
Staring out the windows
Looking out the door
Checking my phone
Wishing you would call
Wishing I was there with you to somehow break
your fall
If only I could turn back time
Take all your heartaches and make them mine
Wishing somehow I could make you see
With a little time how much better things could
be
But you couldn't see that through all of your
pain
And now with you gone things will never be the
same

A sixteen minute phone call on the anniversary
of my birth
A few short days later
You're no longer on this Earth
I pray for you each night
Before I go to sleep
I'm trying to be strong but I often sit and weep
I know that you can hear me now
Much better than before
And that all your pains subsided
You're not hurting anymore
I don't think I'll understand just why you chose
to go
But then again … maybe
that's not for me to know
Your smile your love your laugh your light
Illuminates the path on the darkest of night
So fly high with the angels now
And sing your favorite song
As long as there's a breath in me your memory
lives on

Without You

It appears I've survived my most turbulent days
thus far
Days that rocked my foundation
Days that left a nasty scar
And all the while not knowing
Of the love and care people were showing
Until the day after resting
When silence was screaming and patience was
testing
The day I was able to take a deep breath
Pull myself together and finally reflect
On all the hugs and tears
Letting go of deepest fears
Conversations in the dark

Help to mend a broken heart
It wasn't just me that got me through
Because there's no me without each one of you